Tertullian
On the Pallium

Tertullian
On the Pallium

Tertullian
On the Pallium

© Lighthouse Publishing 2018

All rights reserved. Without limiting the rights under copyright reserved above, no part of this publication may be reproduced, stored in a retrieval system, or transmitted, in any form or by any means (electronic, mechanical, photocopying, recording or otherwise), without the prior written permission of the copyright owner of this book.

Published by
Lighthouse Christian Publishing
SAN 257-4330
5531 Dufferin Drive
Savage, Minnesota, 55378
United States of America

www.lighthousechristianpublishing.com

Tertullian

On the Pallium.

Chapter I.- Time Changes Nations' Dresses—and Fortunes.

    Men of Carthage, ever princes of Africa, ennobled by ancient memories, blest with modern felicities, I rejoice that times are so prosperous with you that you have leisure to spend and pleasure to find in criticizing dress. These are the "piping times of peace" and plenty. Blessings rain from the empire and from the sky. Still, you too of old time wore your garments—your tunics—of another shape; and indeed they were in repute for the skill of the weft, and the harmony of the hue, and the due proportion of the size, in that they were neither prodigally long across the shins, nor immodestly scanty between the knees, nor niggardly to the arms, nor tight to the hands, but, without being shadowed by even a girdle arranged to divide the folds, they stood on men's backs with quadrate symmetry. The garment of the mantle extrinsically—itself too quadrangular—thrown back on either shoulder, and meeting closely round the neck in the gripe of the buckle, used to repose on the shoulders. Its counterpart is now the priestly dress, sacred to Æsculapius, whom you now call your own. So, too, in your immediate vicinity, the sister State used to clothe (her citizens); and wherever else in Africa Tyre (has settled). But when the

On the Pallium

urn of worldly lots varied, and God favored the Romans, the sister State, indeed, of her own choice hastened to affect a change; in order that when Scipio put in at her ports she might already beforehand have greeted him in the way of dress, precocious in her Romanizing. To you, however, after the benefit in which your injury resulted, as exempting you from the infinity of age, not (deposing you) from your height of eminence, —after Gracchus and his foul omens, after Lepidus and his rough jests, after Pompeius and his triple altars, and Cæsar and his long delays, when Statilius Taurus reared your ramparts, and Sentius Saturninus pronounced the solemn form of your inauguration, —while concord lends her aid, the gown is offered. Well! what a circuit has it taken! from Pelasgians to Lydians; from Lydians to Romans: in order that from the shoulders of the sublimer people it should descend to embrace Carthaginians! Henceforth, finding your tunic too long, you suspend it on a dividing cincture; and the redundancy of your now smooth toga you support by gathering it together fold upon fold; and, with whatever other garment social condition or dignity or season clothes you, the mantle, at any rate, which used to be worn by all ranks and conditions among you, you not only are unmindful of, but even deride. For my own part, I wonder not (thereat), in the face of a more ancient evidence (of your forgetfulness). For the ram withal—not that which Laberius (calls) "Back-twisted-horned, wool-skinned, stones-dragging," but a beam-like engine it is, which does military service in battering walls—never before poised by any, the redoubted Carthage, "Keenest in pursuits of war," is said to have been the first of all to have equipped for the oscillatory work of pendulous impetus; modelling the power of her engine after the choleric fury of the head-avenging beast. When, however, their country's fortunes are at the last gasp, and the ram, now turned Roman, is doing his deeds of daring against the ramparts which erst were his own, forthwith the Carthaginians stood dumbfounded as at a "novel" and "strange" ingenuity: "so much doth Time's long age avail to change!" Thus, in short, it is that the mantle, too, is not recognized.

Chapter II. —The Law of Change, or Mutation, Universal.

Draw we now our material from some other source, lest Punichood either blush or else grieve in the midst of Romans. To change her habit is, at all events, the stated function of entire nature. The very world itself (this which we inhabit) meantime discharges it. See to it Anaximander, if he thinks there are more (worlds): see to it, whoever else (thinks there exists another) anywhere at the region of the Meropes, as Silenus prates in the ears of Midas, apt (as those ears are), it must be admitted, for even huger fables. Nay, even if Plato thinks there exists one of which this of ours is the image, that likewise must necessarily have similarly to undergo mutation; inasmuch as, if it is a "world," it will consist of diverse substances and offices, answerable to the form of that which is here the "world:" for "world" it will not be if it be not just as the "world" is. Things which, in diversity, tend to unity, are diverse by demutation. In short, it is their vicissitudes which federate the discord of their diversity. Thus it will be by mutation that every "world" will exist whose corporate structure is the result of diversities, and whose attemperation is the result of vicissitudes. At all events, this hostelry of ours is versiform, —a fact which is patent to eyes that are closed, or utterly Homeric. Day and night revolve in turn. The sun varies by annual stations, the moon by monthly phases. The stars— distinct in their confusion—sometimes drop, sometimes resuscitate, somewhat. The circuit of the heaven is now resplendent with serenity, now dismal with cloud; or else rain-showers come rushing down, and whatever missiles (mingle) with them: thereafter (follows) a slight sprinkling, and then again brilliance. So, too, the sea has an ill repute for honesty; while at one time, the breezes equably swaying it, tranquility gives it the semblance of probity, calm gives it the semblance of even temper; and then all of a sudden it heaves restlessly with mountain-waves. Thus, too, if you survey the earth, loving to clothe herself seasonably, you would nearly be ready to deny her identity, when, remembering her green, you behold her yellow, and will ere long see her hoary too. Of the rest of her adornment also, what is there which is not subject to interchanging mutation—the higher ridges of her mountains by decursion, the veins of her fountains by disappearance, and the pathways of her streams by alluvial formation? There was a time when her whole orb, withal, underwent mutation, overrun by all waters. To this day marine conchs and tritons' horns sojourn as foreigners on the mountains, eager to prove to Plato that even the heights have undulated. But withal, by ebbing out, her orb again underwent a formal mutation; another, but the same. Even now her shape undergoes local mutations, when (some particular) spot is damaged; when among her islands Delos is now no more, Samos a heap of sand, and the Sibyl (is thus proved) no liar; when in the Atlantic (the isle) that was equal in size to Libya or Asia is sought in vain; when formerly a side of Italy, severed to the center by the shivering shock of the Adriatic and the Tyrrhenian seas, leaves Sicily as its relics; when that total swoop of discission, whirling backwards the contentious encounters of the mains, invested the sea with a novel vice, the vice not of spewing out wrecks, but of devouring them! The continent as well suffers from heavenly or else from inherent forces. Glance at Palestine. Where Jordan's river is the arbiter of boundaries, (behold) a vast waste, and a bereaved region, and bootless land! And once (there were there) cities, and flourishing peoples, and the soil yielded its fruits. Afterwards, since God is a Judge, impiety earned showers of fire: Sodom's day is over, and Gomorrah is no more; and all is ashes; and the neighbor sea no less than the soil experiences a living death! Such a cloud overcast Etruria, burning down her ancient Volsinii, to teach Campania (all the more by the eruption of her Pompeii) to look expectantly upon her own mountains. But far be (the repetition of such catastrophes)! Would that Asia, withal, were by this time without cause for anxiety about the soil's voracity! Would, too, that Africa had once for all quailed before the devouring chasm, expiated by the treacherous absorption of one single camp! Many other such detriments besides have made innovations upon the fashion of our orb, and moved (particular) spots (in it). Very great also has been the license of wars. But it is no less irksome to recount sad details than (to recount) the vicissitudes of kingdoms, (and to show) how frequent have been their mutations, from Ninus the progeny of Belus, onwards; if indeed Ninus was the first to have a kingdom, as the ancient profane authorities assert. Beyond his time the pen is not wont (to travel), in general, among you (heathens). From the Assyrians, it may be, the histories of "recorded time" begin to open. We, however, who are habitual readers of divine histories, are masters of the subject from the nativity of the universe itself. But I prefer, at the present time, joyous details, inasmuch as things joyous withal are subject to mutation. In short, whatever the sea has washed away, the heaven burned down, the earth undermined, the sword shorn down, reappears at some other time by the turn of compensation. For in primitive days not only was the earth, for the greater part of her circuit, empty and uninhabited; but if any particular race had seized upon any part, it existed for itself alone. And so, understanding at last that all things worshipped themselves, (the earth) consulted to weed and scrape her copiousness (of inhabitants), in one place densely packed, in another abandoning their posts; in order that thence (as it were from grafts and settings) peoples from peoples, cities from cities, might be planted throughout every region of her orb. Transmigrations were made by the swarms of redundant races. The exuberance of the Scythians fertilizes the Persians; the Phœnicians gush out into Africa; the Phrygians give birth to the Romans; the seed of the Chaldeans is led out into Egypt; subsequently, when transferred thence, it becomes the Jewish race. So, too, the posterity of Hercules, in likewise, proceed to occupy the Peloponnesus for the behoove of Temenus. So, again, the Ionian comrades of Neleus furnish Asia with new cities: so, again, the Corinthians with Archias, fortify Syracuse. But antiquity is by this time a vain thing (to refer to), when our own careers are before our eyes. How large a portion of our orb has the present age reformed! how many cities has the triple power of our existing empire either produced, or else augmented, or else restored! While God favors so many Augusti unitedly, how many populations have been transferred to other localities! how many peoples reduced! how many orders restored to their ancient splendor! how many barbarians baffled! In truth, our orb is the admirably cultivated estate of this empire; every aconite of hostility eradicated; and the cactus and bramble of clandestinely crafty familiarity wholly uptorn; and (the orb itself) delightsome beyond the orchard of Alcinoüs and the rosary of Midas. Praising, therefore, our orbin its mutations, why do you point the finger of scorn at a man?

Chapter III. —Beasts Similarly Subject to the Law of Mutation.

Beasts, too, instead of a garment, change their form. And yet the peacock withal has plumage for a garment, and a garment indeed of the choicest; nay, in the bloom of his neck richer than any purple, and in the effulgence of his back more gilded than any edging, and in the sweep of his tail more flowing than any train; many-colored, diverse-colored, and versi-colored; never itself, ever another, albeit ever itself when other; in a word, mutable as oft as moveable. The serpent, too, deserves to be mentioned, albeit not in the same breath as the peacock; for he too wholly changes what has been allotted him—his hide and his age: if it is true, (as it is,) that when he has felt the creeping of old age throughout him, he squeezes himself into confinement; crawls into a cave and out of his skin simultaneously; and, clean shorn on the spot, immediately on crossing the threshold leaves his slough behind him then and there, and uncoils himself in a new youth: with his scales his years, too, are repudiated. The hyena, if you observe, is of an annual sex, alternately masculine and feminine. I say nothing of the stag, because himself withal, the witness of his own age, feeding on the serpent, languishes—from the effect of the poison—into youth. There is, withal,

> "A tardigrade field-haunting quadruped, Humble and rough."

The tortoise of Pacuvius, you think? No. There is another beastling which the versicle fits; in size, one of the moderate exceedingly, but a grand name. If, without previously knowing him, you hear tell of a chameleon, you will at once apprehend something yet more huge united with a lion. But when you stumble upon him, generally in a vineyard, his whole bulk sheltered beneath a vine leaf, you will forthwith laugh at the egregious audacity of the name, inasmuch as there is no moisture even in his body, though in far more minute creatures the body is liquefied. The chameleon is a living pellicle. His headkin begins straight from his spine, for neck he has none: and thus reflection is hard for him; but, in circumspection, his eyes are out darting, nay, they are revolving points of light. Dull and weary, he scarce raises from the ground, but drags, his footstep amazedly, and moves forward, —he rather demonstrates, than takes, a step: ever fasting, to boot, yet never fainting; agape he feeds; heaving, bellows like, he ruminates; his food wind. Yet withal the chameleon is able to affect a total self-mutation, and that is all. For, whereas his color is properly one, yet, whenever anything has approached him, then he blushes. To the chameleon alone has been granted—as our common saying has it—to sport with his own hide.

Much had to be said in order that, after due preparation, we might arrive at man. From whatever beginning you admit him as springing, naked at all events and ungarmented he came from his fashioner's hand: afterwards, at length, without waiting for permission, he possesses himself, by a premature grasp, of wisdom. Then and there hastening to forecover what, in his newly made body, it was not yet due to modesty (to forecover), he surrounds himself meantime with fig-leaves: subsequently, on being driven from the confines of his birthplace because he had sinned, he went, skin clad, to the world as to a mine.

But these are secrets, nor does their knowledge appertain to all. Come, let us hear from your own store— (a store) which the Egyptians narrate, and Alexander digests, and his mother reads—touching the time of Osiris, when Ammon, rich in sheep, comes to him out of Libya. In short, they tell us that Mercury, when among them, delighted with the softness of a ram which he had chanced to stroke, flayed a little ewe; and, while he persistently tries and (as the pliancy of the material invited him) thins out the thread by assiduous traction, wove it into the shape of the pristine net which he had joined with strips of linen. But you have preferred to assign all the management of wool-work and structure of the loom to Minerva; whereas a more diligent workshop was presided over by Arachne. Thenceforth material (was abundant). Nor do I speak of the sheep of Miletus, and Selge, and Altinum, or of those for which Tarentum or Bætica is famous, with nature for their dyer: but (I speak of the fact) that shrubs afford you clothing, and the grassy parts of flax, losing their greenness, turn white by washing. Nor was it enough to plant and sow your tunic, unless it had likewise fallen to your lot to fish for raiment. For the sea withal yields fleeces, inasmuch as the more brilliant shells of a mossy wooliness furnish a hairy stuff. Further: it is no secret that the silkworm—a species of wormling it is—presently reproduces safe and sound (the fleecy threads) which, by drawing them through the air, she distends more skillfully than the dial-like webs of spiders, and then devours. In like manner, if you kill it, the threads which you coil are forthwith instinct with vivid color.

The ingenuities, therefore, of the tailoring art, superadded to, and following up, so abundant a store of materials—first with a view to coveting humanity, where Necessity led the way; and subsequently with a view to adorning withal, ay, and inflating it, where Ambition followed in the wake—have promulgated the various forms of garments. Of which forms, part are worn by particular nations, without being common to the rest; part, on the other hand, universally, as being useful to all: as, for instance, this Mantle, albeit it is more Greek (than Latin), has yet by this time found, in speech, a home in Latium. With the word the garment entered. And accordingly the very man who used to sentence Greeks to extrusion from the city, but learned (when he was now advanced in years) their alphabet and speech—the selfsame Cato, by baring his shoulder at the time of his prætorship, showed no less favor to the Greeks by his mantle-like garb.

Chapter IV. —Change Not Always Improvement.

Why, now, if the Roman fashion is (social) salvation to everyone, are you nevertheless Greek to a degree, even in points not honorable? Or else, if it is not so, whence in the world is it that provinces which have had a better training, provinces which nature adapted rather for surmounting by hard struggling the difficulties of the soil, derive the pursuits of the wrestling-ground—pursuits which fall into a sad old age and labor in vain—and the unction with mud, and the rolling in sand, and the dry dietary? Whence comes it that some of our Numidians, with their long locks made longer by horsetail plumes, learn to bid the barber shave their skin close, and to exempt their crown alone from the knife? Whence comes it that men shaggy and hirsute learn to teach the resin to feed on their arms with such rapacity, the tweezers to weed their chin so thievishly? A prodigy it is, that all this should be done without the Mantle! To the Mantle appertains this whole Asiatic practice! What hast thou, Libya, and thou, Europe, to do with athletic refinements, which thou knows not how to dress? For, in sooth, what kind of thing is it to practice Greekish depilation more than Greekish attire? The transfer of dress approximates to culpability just in so far as it is not custom, but nature, which suffers the change. There is a wide enough difference between the honor due to time, and religion. Let Custom show fidelity to Time, Nature to God. To Nature, accordingly, the Larissæan hero gave a shock by turning into a virgin; he who had been reared on the marrows of wild beasts (whence, too, was derived the composition of his name, because he had been a stranger with his lips to the maternal breast); he who had been reared by a rocky and wood-haunting and monstrous trainer in a stony school. You would bear patiently, if it were in a boy's case, his mother's solicitude; but he at all events was already be-haired, he at all events had already secretly given proof of his manhood to someone, when he consents to wear the flowing stole, to dress his hair, to cultivate his skin, to consult the mirror, to bedizen his neck; effeminated even as to his ear by boring, whereof his bust at Sigeum still retains the trace. Plainly afterwards he turned soldier: for necessity restored him his sex. The clarion had sounded of battle: nor were arms far to seek. "The steel's self," says (Homer), "attracted the hero." Else if, after that incentive as well as before, he had persevered in his maidenhood, he might withal have been married! Behold, accordingly, mutation! A monster, I call him, —a double monster: from man to woman; by and by from woman to man: whereas neither ought the truth to have been belied, nor the deception confessed. Each fashion of changing was evil: the one opposed to nature, the other contrary to safety.

Still more disgraceful was the case when lust transfigured a man in his dress, than when some maternal dread did so: and yet adoration is offered by you to me, whom you ought to blush at, —that Clubshaftandhidebearer, who exchanged for womanly attire the whole proud heritage of his name! Such license was granted to the secret haunts of Lydia, that Hercules was prostituted in the person of Omphale, and Omphale in that of Hercules. Where were Diomed and his gory mangers? where Busiris and his funereal altars? where Geryon, triply one? The club preferred still to reek with their brains when it was being pestered with unguents! The now veteran (stain of the) Hydra's and of the Centaurs' blood upon the shafts was gradually eradicated by the pumice-stone, familiar to the hair-pin! while voluptuousness insulted over the fact that, after transfixing monsters, they should perchance sew a coronet! No sober woman even, or heroine of any note, would have adventured her shoulders beneath the hide of such a beast, unless after long softening and smoothening down and deodorization (which in Omphale's house, I hope, was effected by balsam and fenugreek-salve: I suppose the mane, too, submitted to the comb) for fear of getting her tender neck imbued with lionly toughness. The yawning mouth stuffed with hair, the jaw teeth overshadowed amid the forelocks, the whole outraged visage, would have roared had it been able. Nemea, at all events (if the spot has any presiding genius), groaned: for then she looked around, and saw that she had lost her lion. What sort of being the said Hercules was in Omphale's silk, the description of Omphale in Hercules' hide has inferentially depicted.

But, again, he who had formerly rivalled the Tirynthian—the pugilist Cleomachus—subsequently, at Olympia, after losing by efflux his masculine sex by an incredible mutation—bruised within his skin and without, worthy to be wreathed among the "Fullers" even of Novius, and deservedly commemorated by the mimographer Lentulus in his Catinensians—did, of course, not only cover with bracelets the traces left by (the bands of) the cestus, but likewise supplanted the coarse ruggedness of his athlete's cloak with some superfinely wrought tissue.

Of Physco and Sardanapalus I must be silent, whom, but for their eminence in lusts, no one would recognize as kings. But I must be silent, for fear lest even they set up a muttering concerning some of your Cæsars, equally lost to shame; for fear lest a mandate have been given to canine constancy to point to a Cæsar impurer than Physco, softer than Sardanapalus, and indeed a second Nero.

Nor less warmly does the force of vainglory also work for the mutation of clothing, even while manhood is preserved. Every affection is a heat: when, however, it is blown to (the flame of) affectation, forthwith, by the blaze of glory, it is an ardor. From this fuel, therefore, you see a great king—inferior only to his glory—seething. He had conquered the Median race, and was conquered by Median garb. Doffing the triumphal mail, he degraded himself into the captive trousers! The breast dissculptured with scaly bosses, by covering it with a transparent texture he bared; punting still after the work of war, and (as it were) softening, he extinguished it with the ventilating silk! Not sufficiently swelling of spirit was the Macedonian, unless he had likewise found delight in a highly inflated garb: only that philosophers withal (I believe) themselves affect somewhat of that kind; for I hear that there has been (such a thing as) philosophizing in purple. If a philosopher (appears) in purple, why not in gilded slippers too? For a Tyrian to be shod in anything but gold, is by no means consonant with Greek habits. Someone will say, "Well, but there was another who wore silk indeed, and shod himself in brazen sandals." Worthily, indeed, in order that at the bottom of his Bacchantian raiment he might make some tinkling sound, did he walk in cymbals! But if, at that moment, Diogenes had been barking from his tub, he would not (have trodden on him) with muddy feet—as the Platonic couches testify—but would have carried Empedocles down bodily to the secret recesses of the Cloacinæ; in order that he who had madly thought himself a celestial being might, as a god, salute first his sisters, and afterwards men. Such garments, therefore, as alienate from nature and modesty, let it be allowed to be just to eye fixedly and point at with the finger and expose to ridicule by a nod. Just so, if a man were to wear a dainty robe trailing on the ground with Menander like effeminacy, he would hear applied to himself that which the comedian says, "What sort of a cloak is that maniac wasting?" For, now that the contracted brow of censorial vigilance is long since smoothed down, so far as reprehension is concerned, promiscuous usage offers to our gaze freedmen in equestrian garb, branded slaves in that of gentlemen, the notoriously infamous in that of the freeborn, clowns in that of city-folk, buffoons in that of lawyers, rustics in regimentals; the corpse-bearer, the pimp, the gladiator trainer, clothe themselves as you do. Turn, again, to women. You have to behold what Cæcina Severus pressed upon the grave attention of the senate—matrons stoleless in public. In fact, the penalty inflicted by the decrees of the augur Lentulus upon any matron who had thus cashiered herself was the same as for fornication; inasmuch as certain matrons had sedulously promoted the disuse of garments which were the evidences and guardians of dignity, as being impediments to the practicing of prostitution. But now, in their self-prostitution, in order that they may the more readily be approached, they have abjured stole, and chemise, and bonnet, and cap; yes, and even the very litters and sedans in which they used to be kept in privacy and secrecy even in public. But while one extinguishes her proper adornments, another blazes forth such as are not hers. Look at the street-walkers, the shambles of popular lusts; also at the female self-abusers with their sex; and, if it is better to withdraw your eyes from such shameful spectacles of publicly slaughtered chastity, yet do but look with eyes askance, (and) you will at once see (them to be) matrons! And, while the overseer of brothels airs her swelling silk, and consoles her neck—more impure than her haunt—with necklaces, and inserts in the armlets (which even matrons themselves would, of the guerdons bestowed upon brave men, without hesitation have appropriated) hands privy to all that is shameful, (while) she fits on her impure leg the pure white or pink shoe; why do you not stare at such garbs? or, again, at those which falsely plead religion as the supporter of their novelty? while for the sake of an all-white dress, and the distinction of a fillet, and the privilege of a helmet, some are initiated into (the mysteries of) Ceres; while, on account of an opposite hankering after somber raiment, and a gloomy woolen covering upon the head, others run mad in Bellona's temple; while the attraction of surrounding themselves with a tunic more broadly striped with purple, and casting over their shoulders a cloak of Galatian scarlet, commends Saturn (to the affections of others). When this Mantle itself, arranged with more rigorous care, and sandals after the Greek model, serve to flatter Æsculapius, how much more should you then accuse and assail it with your eyes, as being guilty of superstition—albeit superstition simple and unaffected? Certainly, when first it clothes this wisdom which renounces superstitions with all their vanities, then most assuredly is the Mantle, above all the garments in which you array your gods and goddesses, an august robe; and, above all the caps and tufts of your Salii and Flamines, a sacerdotal attire. Lower your eyes, I advise you, (and) reverence the garb, on the one ground, meantime, (without waiting for others,) of being a renouncer of your error.

Chapter V.—Virtues of the Mantle. It Pleads in Its Own Defense.

"Still," say you, "must we thus change from gown to Mantle?" Why, what if from diadem and scepter? Did Anacharsis change otherwise, when to the royalty of Scythia he preferred philosophy? Grant that there be no (miraculous) signs in proof of your transformation for the better: there is somewhat which this your garb can do. For, to begin with the simplicity of its up taking: it needs no tedious arrangement. Accordingly, there is no necessity for any artist formally to dispose its wrinkled folds from the beginning a day beforehand, and then to reduce them to a more finished elegance, and to assign to the guardianship of the stretchers the

whole figment of the massed boss; subsequently, at daybreak, first gathering up by the aid of a girdle the tunic which it were better to have woven of more moderate length (in the first instance), and, again scrutinizing the boss, and rearranging any disarrangement, to make one part prominent on the left, but (making now an end of the folds) to draw backwards from the shoulders the circuit of it whence the hollow is formed, and, leaving the right shoulder free, heap it still upon the left, with another similar set of folds reserved for the back, and thus clothe the man with a burden! In short, I will persistently ask your own conscience, what is your first sensation in wearing your gown? Do you feel yourself clad, or laded? wearing a garment, or carrying it? If you shall answer negatively, I will follow you home; I win see what you hasten to do immediately after crossing your threshold. There is really no garment the doffing whereof congratulates a man more than the gown's does. Of shoes we say nothing—implements as they are of torture proper to the gown, most uncleanly protection to the feet, yes, and false too. For who would not find it expedient, in cold and heat, to stiffen with feet bare rather than in a shoe with feet bound? A mighty munition for the tread have the Venetian shoe-factories provided in the shape of effeminate boots! Well, but, than the Mantle nothing is more expedite, even if it be double, like that of Crates. Nowhere is there a compulsory waste of time in dressing yourself (in it), seeing that its whole art consists in loosely covering. That can be effected by a single circumjection, and one in no case inelegant: thus it wholly covers every part of the man at once.
The shoulder it either exposes or encloses: in other respects it adheres to the shoulder; it has no surrounding support; it has no surrounding tie; it has no anxiety as to the fidelity with which its folds keep their place; easily it manages, easily readjusts itself: even in the doffing it is consigned to no cross until the morrow. If any shirt is worn beneath it, the torment of a girdle is superfluous: if anything in the way of shoeing is worn, it is a most cleanly work; or else the feet are rather bare, —more

manly, at all events, (if bare,) than in shoes. These (pleas I advance) for the Mantle in the meantime, in so far as you have defamed it by name. Now, however, it challenges you on the score of its function withal. "I," it says, "owe no duty to the forum, the election-ground, or the senate-house; I keep no obsequious vigil, preoccupy no platforms, hover about no prætorian residences; I am not odorant of the canals, am not odorant of the lattices, am no constant wearer out of benches, no wholesale router of laws, no barking pleader, no judge, no soldier, no king: I have withdrawn from the populace. My only business is with myself: except that other care I have none, save not to care. The better life you would more enjoy in seclusion than in publicity. But you will decry me as indolent. Forsooth, 'we are to live for our country, and empire, and estate.' Such used, of old, to be the sentiment. None is born for another, being destined to die for himself. At all events, when we come to the Epicuri and Zenones, you give the epithet of 'sages' to the whole teacherhood of Quietude, who have consecrated that Quietude with the name of 'supreme' and 'unique' pleasure. Still, to some extent it will be allowed, even to me, to confer benefit on the public. From any and every boundary-stone or altar it is my wont to prescribe medicines to morals—medicines which will be more felicitous in conferring good health upon public affairs, and states, and empires, than your works are. Indeed, if I proceed to encounter you with naked foils, gowns have done the commonwealth more hurt than cuirasses. Moreover, I flatter no vices; I give quarter to no lethargy, no slothful encrustation. I apply the cauterizing iron to the ambition which led M. Tullius to buy a circular table of citron-wood for more than £4000, and Asinius Gallus to pay twice as much for an ordinary table of the same Moorish wood (Hem! at what fortunes did they value woody dapplings!), or, again, Sulla to frame dishes of a hundred pounds' weight. I fear lest that balance be small, when a Drusillanus (and he withal a slave of Claudius!) constructs a tray of the weight of 500 lbs.! —a tray indispensable, perchance, to the aforesaid tables, for which, if a workshop was erected, there ought to have been erected a dining room too. Equally do I plunge the scalpel into the inhumanity which led Vedius Pollio to expose slaves to fill the bellies of sea-eels. Delighted, forsooth, with his novel savagery, he kept land-monsters, toothless, clawless, hornless: it was his pleasure to turn perforce into wild beasts his fish, which (of course) were to be forthwith cooked, that in their entrails he himself withal might taste some savor of the bodies of his own slaves. I will forelop the gluttony which led Hortensius the orator to be the first to have the heart to slay a peacock for the sake of food; which led Aufidius Lurco to be the first to vitiate meat with stuffing, and by the aid of forcemeats to raise them to an adulterous flavor; which led Asinius Celer to purchase the viand of a single mullet at nearly £50;73 which led Æsopus the actor to preserve in his pantry a dish of the value of nearly £800, made up of birds of the selfsame costliness (as the mullet aforesaid), consisting of all the songsters and talkers; which led his son, after such a titbit, to have the hardihood to hunger after somewhat yet more sumptuous: for he swallowed down pearls—costly even on the ground of their name—I suppose for fear he should have supped more beggarly than his father. I am silent as to the Neros and Apicii and Rufi. I will give a cathartic to the impurity of a Scaurus, and the gambling of a Curius, and the intemperance of an Antony. And remember that these, out of the many (whom I have named), were men of the toga—such as among the men of the pallium you would not easily find. These purulencies of a state who will eliminate and exsuppurate, save a bemantled speech?

Chapter VI. —Further Distinctions, and Crowning Glory, of the Pallium.

"'With speech,' says (my antagonist), 'you have tried to persuade me,—a most sage medicament.' But, albeit utterance be mute—impeded by infancy or else checked by bashfulness, for life is content with an even tongueless philosophy—my very cutis eloquent. A philosopher, in fact, is heard so long as he is seen. My very sight puts vices to the blush. Who suffers not, when he sees his own rival? Who can bear to gaze ocularly at him at whom mentally he cannot? Grand is the benefit conferred by the Mantle, at the thought whereof moral improbity absolutely blushes. Let philosophy now see to the question of her own profitableness; for she is not the only associate whom I boast. Other scientific arts of public utility I boast. From my store are clothed the first teacher of the forms of letters, the first explainer of their sounds, the first trainer in the rudiments of arithmetic, the grammarian, the rhetorician, the sophist, the medical man, the poet, the musical timebeater, the astrologer, and the bird gazer. All that is liberal in studies is covered by my four angles. 'True; but all these rank lower than Roman knights' Well; but your gladiatorial trainers, and all their ignominious following, are conducted into the arena in togas. This, no doubt, will be the indignity implied in 'From gown to Mantle!'" Well, so speaks the Mantle. But I confer on it likewise a fellowship with a divine sect and discipline. Joy, Mantle, and exult! A better philosophy has now deigned to honor thee, ever since thou hast begun to be a Christian's vesture!

Elucidations.

I.

(The garment...too quadrangular, p. 5.)

Speaking of the Greek priests of Korfou, the erudite Bishop of Lincoln, lately deceased, has remarked, "There is something very picturesque in the appearance of these persons, with their black caps resembling the modius seen on the heads of the ancient statues of Serapis and Osiris, their long beards and pale complexions, and their black flowing cloak, —a relic, no doubt, of the old ecclesiastical garment of which Tertullian wrote." These remarks are illustrated by an engraving on the same page.

He thus identifies the pallium with the gown of Justin Martyr; nor can there be any reasonable doubt that the pallium of the West was the counterpart of the Greek φελόνιον and of the φαιλόνη, which St. Paul left at Troas. Endearing associations have clung to it from the mention of this apostolic cloak in Holy Scripture. It doubtless influenced Justin in giving his philosopher's gown a new significance, and the modern Greeks insist that such was the apparel of the apostles. The seamless robe of Christ Himself belongs to Him only.

Tertullian rarely acknowledges his obligations to other Doctors; but Justin's example and St. Paul's cloak must have been in his thoughts when he rejected the toga, and claimed the pallium, as a Christian's attire. Our Edinburgh translator has assumed that it was the "ascetics' mantle," and perhaps it was. Our author wished to make all Christians ascetics, like himself, and hence his enthusiasm for a distinctive costume. Anyhow, "the Doctor's gown" of the English universities, which is also used among the Gallicans and in Savoy, is one of the most ancient as well as dignified vestments in ecclesiastical use; and for the prophetic or preaching function of the clergy it is singularly appropriate.

"The pallium," says a learned author, the late Wharton B. Marriott of Oxford, "is the Greek ἱμάτιον, the outer garment or wrapper worn occasionally by persons of all conditions of life. It corresponded in general use to the Roman toga, but in the earlier Roman language, that of republican times, was as distinctively suggestive of a Greek costume as the toga of that of Rome." To Tertullian, therefore, his preference for the pallium was doubtless commended by all these considerations; and the distinctively Greek character of Christian theology was indicated also by his choice. He loved the learning of Alexandria, and reflected the spirit of the East.

II.

(Superstition, p. 10, near note 9.)

The pall afterwards imposed upon Anglican and other primates by the Court of Rome was at first a mere complimentary present from the patriarchal see of the West. It became a badge of dependence and of bondage (obsta principiis). Only the ornamental bordering was sent, "made of lamb's-wool and superstition," says old Fuller, for whose amusing remarks see his Church Hist., vol. i. p. 179, ed. 1845. Rome gives primitive names to middle-age corruptions: needless to say the "pall" of her court is nothing like the pallium of our author.

www.ingramcontent.com/pod-product-compliance
Lightning Source LLC
Chambersburg PA
CBHW052046070526
44584CB00018B/2635